WHO WERE THE FIRST PEOPLE?

Phil Roxbee Cox & Struan Reid

Illustrated by Gerald Wood

Designed by Diane Thistlethwaite
& Vicki Groombridge

Cover design: Russell Punter
Cover illustration: Inklink Firenze
History consultants: Nick Merriman & Anne Millard
Research assistant: Georgina Andrews
Series editor: Jane Chisolm

CONTENTS

Who were the first people?

No one knows for sure. They lived such a long time ago. But scientists believe people have been around for about two million years.

The funny sounding names are ones that scientists have given these types of people. The words are written in a language called Latin.

What did they look like?

A little different from us. Most scientists believe that very early people, animals and plants have changed, or evolved, into modern people, animals and plants. This is called evolution.

This picture shows a few stages in the evolution of people.

This is when each type first appeared on Earth.

Ramapithecus — 14 million years ago

Homo erectus — 1.7 million years ago

Homo sapiens — 400,000 years ago

Homo sapiens sapiens (the first 'true' humans) — 100,000 years ago

What did the first people eat?

They fed themselves by gathering plants and, later, by hunting animals for food. Scientists call them "hunter-gatherers".

Key:

1 Horse	12 Homo habilis
2 Wolf	13 Megaloceros
3 Farmer	14 Sthenurus
4 Goat	15 Glyptodon
5 Giant sloth	16 Diatryma
6 Teratornis	17 Ape
7 Sabre-toothed tiger	18 Phrotherium
8 Woolly rhino	19 Bat
9 Macrauchenia	20 Baluchitherium
10 Mammoth	21 Arsinoitherium
11 Homo sapiens	22 Pachyrukhos
	23 Basilosaurus

These animals are walking, swimming or flying along a "time line" in groups. The farther to the right their group is, the farther back in time they are. Look at the key to find out what they were called.

First appeared 4,000 to 10,000 years ago

What does "prehistoric" mean?

"Before history". This was the time before people left any books or writings behind. Prehistory lasted for millions of years. It's much longer than history.

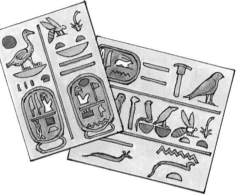

This is an example of some of the earliest writing ever found. It is about 5,000 years old.

How do we know anything about prehistoric people?

Only through the hard work of archaeologists. These are people who seek out, dig up and study very old objects and remains.

This object was found by archaeologists. What is it? A knife? A comb?

Stone spearhead. The wooden shaft will rot away over time.

This prehistoric boy is learning to make spears by watching his big brother.

By comparing it with earlier finds, and studying things near it, archaeologists realized the object was a spearhead.

First appeared 2 million to 54 million years ago

First appeared 4,000 to 2 million years ago

There are more of us on the next page.

3

Where in the world did they live?

All over the place. Some of our earliest ancestors probably came from Africa. By about 1.5 million years ago, people were living in the Middle East too.

Half a million years after that, people lived in Europe and Asia.

Of course, these places didn't have these names then. There were no such things as countries.

How did they reach these places?

They walked. In fact, hunter-gatherers walked just about everywhere.

A group of them might have walked a few miles and settled in a new place.

When their children grew up, this new generation might then move on a few more miles.

A boat made from a tree trunk.

This woman has aching feet.

This baby is enjoying the ride.

This group of prehistoric people has been on the move for months without bumping into anyone else.

How many people were there in prehistoric times?

There were probably only twenty or thirty thousand of the first "true" human beings in the whole world. (Scientists call them *Homo sapiens sapiens*.)

This may sound like quite a crowd, but today there are about six billion people on the planet.

First appeared 54 million to 135 million years ago

Were they stupid?

Certainly not. Today, people build on and improve ideas, inventions and discoveries made by people from earlier times. The earliest people had to find out everything for themselves.

How big were their brains?

The more advanced our ancestors became, the bigger brains they had. We know this because the fossils of the skulls of very early people are smaller than later human skulls.

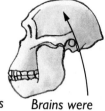

This fossilized skull was once on the neck of an early man. There wasn't much room for his brain in this skull.

Brains were inside this part.

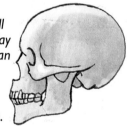

This is an early Homo sapiens skull. The domed area on top had room for a much bigger brain inside it.

This is the skull of a modern day woman. You can see that her skull is much bigger to fit her large brain.

This is the end of the "time line" that started at the bottom of page 2. It has taken us right back through time to the very first insect. The names of the animals on these two pages are in the yellow box.

Key

1 Coryphodon	12 Archaeopteryx	22 Meganeura
2 Ectoconos	13 Compsogathus	23 Sea Lillies
3 Oxyaena	14 Turrilites	24 Edaphosaurus
4 Uintatherium	15 Corythosaurus	25 Millerosaurus
5 Coelanth	16 Dimorphodon	26 Cockroach
6 Hyracotherium	17 Diplodocus	27 Ichthyostega
7 Dimetrodon	18 Saltobosuchus	28 Cystoid
8 Pteranodon	19 Ichtyosaur	29 Stelleroid
9 Plesiosaurs	20 Stegosaurus	30 Sea Scorpion
10 T-Rex	21 Ammonite	31 Trilobite
11 Triceratops		

First appeared 135 million to 225 million years ago

First appeared 225 million to 550 million years ago

What did they look like?

No one knows for sure. Our earliest ancestors didn't paint detailed pictures of each other, or take photographs, so we have very few clues. Most ideas of what they looked like come from studying their remains.

This scene shows some of our early ancestors back from a cold day's hunting.

This tiny carving of a person's head is over 25,000 years old.

Harpoon for spearing fish

This boy wants his supper.

Animal fur

Shells for decoration

It is cold outside, so this fire is needed to keep them warm.

Like all the scenes in this book, this one is based on archaeologists' ideas of what life was like in the past.

Clothes made from animal skins

This girl will go hunting with her parents when she is older.

Were they smaller than us?

Not really. People used to think so because of an early *Homo sapiens* man's skeleton. It was later realized that he wasn't "typical" at all. He had an illness called arthritis, which made him hunched up, and look smaller!

Did they really dress like Tarzan?

No. The first people lived at a time we call the Ice Age. It not only sounds very cold, it *was* very cold. Skimpy loin cloths, like Tarzan's, wouldn't have kept them warm enough.

This early Homo sapiens is only slightly shorter than the much more modern man standing behind him.

6

Internet link: for a link to a Web site where you can find out about a 5,000-year-old Iceman, go to **www.usborne-quicklinks.com**

Did they bother to cut their hair?

Probably. Carvings of heads have been found, showing people with quite fancy hairstyles.

How often they washed their hair is another matter.

These carvings show two very different hairstyles.

What did they make necklaces out of?

All sorts of things. Mainly fossils, shells, teeth and bones.

This shell and bone necklace would have been a treasured possession.

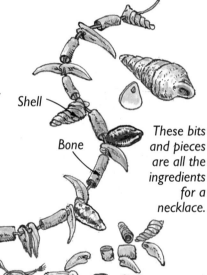

Shell

Bone

These bits and pieces are all the ingredients for a necklace.

Did they wear jewels?

Not precious gems. But they did wear necklaces, pendants and earrings made from other things.

Shell earring

This prehistoric comb is made from animal bone.

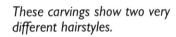

Did you know?

Only a human's thumb can touch the fingertips of the same hand. (Not even apes can do this.) This is why it's much easier for humans to use tools.

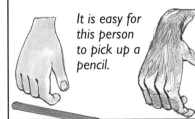

It is easy for this person to pick up a pencil.

The shape of this ape's thumb makes picking things up much harder.

Are archaeologists ever fooled?

Yes, they're only human. In 1913, a skull was found at a place called Piltdown in England. It had the head shape of a man, but the jaw shape of an ape.

Archaeologists were very excited. 40 years later, it was proved to be a trick. Someone had attached an orangutan's jaw to a human skull!

Human skull

Orangutan's jaw

7

Did they really live in caves?

Some early people did, but most couldn't. Unlike houses, caves can't be built, and there weren't enough to go around.

Those who were lucky enough to find a cave lived near the opening. Inside a cave, it was dark and there was no chimney to let out the smoke and smells.

These remains of a prehistoric home have been uncovered by archaeologists.

How do we know all this?

From the work of archaeologists who study remains of our ancestors' homes. You can find out more on pages 30 and 31.

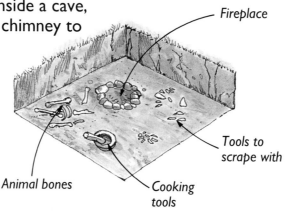

Fireplace

Tools to scrape with

Animal bones

Cooking tools

This shows a settlement of hunter-gatherers.

This reindeer will supply a family with food, clothes and tools.

These men are building a tent. One of them is smiling because it will be his new home.

Branches

All the dead animals' flesh is being scraped off the skins so they can be used for clothes.

A bump on the head

Animal skins for the walls

Firewood

8

Did they have wallpaper?

No, they didn't have any kind of paper. But they did sometimes paint pictures on cave walls. These were usually in the difficult-to-get-to inner parts of the caves, where people didn't actually live. They were often pictures of the animals they hunted.

What are these animals?

This copy of cave paintings shows two animals. Do you know what type of animals they are supposed to be?

What were these inner caves for?

Special occasions. They were probably seen as magical places, doors to another world. People think that they were used by hunters for special ceremonies.

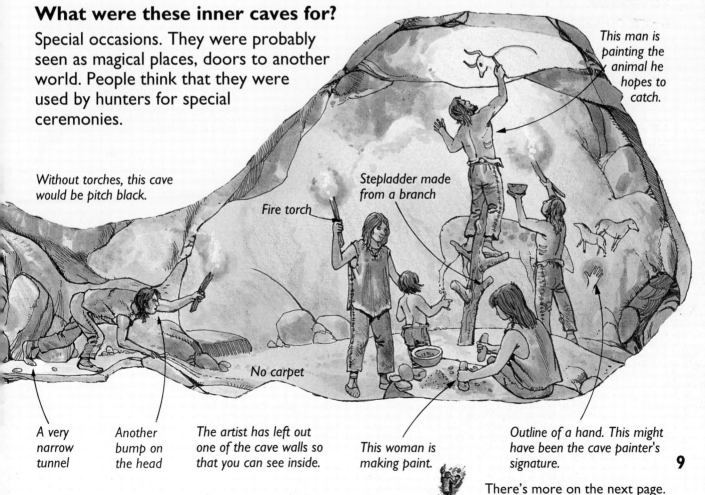

Without torches, this cave would be pitch black.

Fire torch

Stepladder made from a branch

This man is painting the animal he hopes to catch.

No carpet

A very narrow tunnel

Another bump on the head

The artist has left out one of the cave walls so that you can see inside.

This woman is making paint.

Outline of a hand. This might have been the cave painter's signature.

9

There's more on the next page.

Internet link: for a link to a Web site where you can see a mammoth bone house and hear some mammoth bone music, go to **www.usborne-quicklinks.com**

If they didn't live in caves, where did they live?

Hunter-gatherers built small tent-shaped homes like the ones below. They used sticks, grass, skin and bones. Often, these tents were packed full of people.

The walls of this house are made out of grass covered with mud. This makes it warm and waterproof inside.

Shelters like this one were built about 400,000 years ago. It was made from thin branches and bundles of twigs.

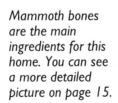

Mammoth bones are the main ingredients for this home. You can see a more detailed picture on page 15.

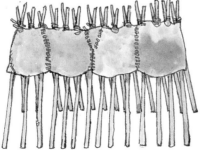

This is a very simple home. It is made of branches and animal skins. It'll need a few more skins on it to keep the rain out.

How did they keep warm?

With plenty of people crammed into very small houses, the heat from everyone's bodies probably helped. Even so, most prehistoric houses would have been pretty cold. Some people made fires inside their homes. Clothes kept them warm too!

This group of people in the scene below are hunter-gatherers. They have set up home by a river for a few months. When the weather gets colder, they will be moving on.

Animal skin walls

Heavy stones hold skins in place.

This hole hasn't been made by a wild animal, but by the artist. This is so that you can see the fire inside the house.

Did they live in towns?

Not for thousands of years. People only began to settle down about 11,000 years ago. Although hunter-gatherers put up their houses in groups, they still moved from place to place.

Did they keep pets?

No. In fact, very early hunter-gatherers would have killed any animal they came across. Then eaten it. Later, they must have realized that dogs could help them hunt.

A stick

The father and mother of these puppies go hunting with the father and mother of this girl.

Food was too precious to share with animals which did not earn it. Even very early farmers, of 11,000 years ago, kept animals as workers and not as lazy pets.

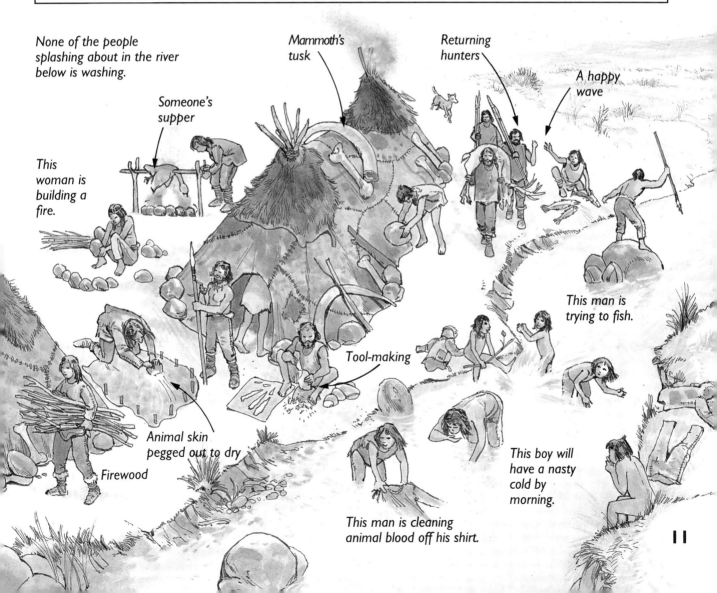

None of the people splashing about in the river below is washing.

Mammoth's tusk

Returning hunters

A happy wave

Someone's supper

This woman is building a fire.

This man is trying to fish.

Tool-making

Animal skin pegged out to dry

Firewood

This boy will have a nasty cold by morning.

This man is cleaning animal blood off his shirt.

Did they hunt dinosaurs?

No, no, no and no again. They were as likely to see a dinosaur wandering around then as we are today.

Dinosaurs died out about 62 million years *before* the first people walked on the Earth. They wouldn't even have known what dinosaurs were.

So what did they eat?

Hunter-gatherers ate wild plants, nuts, fruit, shellfish and any animals they could catch and kill.

Exactly what they ate depended on where in the world they lived.

These people are collecting shellfish off the rocks in the shallow water.

Her job is to open the shells.

This prehistoric cave painting shows a hunter using his (or her) bow and arrow to kill a reindeer.

How did they hunt?

On foot, and with their bare hands to begin with. Later, spears were invented. Then, hundreds of thousands of years after that, they hunted with bows and arrows.

Did they go fishing?

Yes, but not with fishing rods and lines. They would have used their hands, spears and, later, nets.

Did they eat chocolate?

No, but they probably liked sweet-tasting things. There was no sugar, but honey made by wild bees would have been popular.

This ancient picture shows a woman climbing a tree to reach honey in a beehive.

Internet link: for a link to a Web site where you can find out more about food and hunting, go to **www.usborne-quicklinks.com**

Harpoon

Spearheads

Arrowhead

How do we know what they ate?

By studying the seeds and animal bones they left behind which archaeologists have found.

What sort of weapons did they use?

All sorts. (You'll find some examples on pages 17 and 18.) Spears were usually thrown to kill the animal. Knives and axes were used to cut up the meat.

This man is pretending to make a bone tool. He is really about to have a nap.

Once an animal is killed, it is put to good use. Its flesh is eaten, its skin worn, and its bones used for tools.

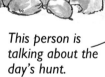

Meat is cooked to make it less chewy and nicer to taste.

These pots are far more modern than the main scene. They are only about 10,000 years old.

Did you know?

Some rubbery tree resin was found in the mouth of a 9,000 year old teenager. Archaeologists think it was a form of chewing gum. Plants were also used as medicines.

Catmint was supposed to make colds better.

This person is talking about the day's hunt.

Eggs

Dandelions

Nuts

Rue might have been used to cure headaches.

Were any of our early ancestors vegetarians?

Yes, the very first ones. People would have eaten what they could find. Later they hunted and ate animals, as well as fruit and vegetables.

There's more on the next page.

What were mammoths?

Huge animals, hunted by our ancestors. They were a type of elephant with long, curvy tusks. Mammoths used their tusks to clear away snow and dig up plants to eat. Their remains have been found all around the world. Mammoths were very woolly.

Why were they so woolly?

They lived in the Ice Age. Unlike elephants today (which live in the warm climates of Africa and India), mammoths needed their long, thick hair and layers of fat to keep warm.

Hunters sneak up behind a large male mammoth. The tips of their spears are long and sharp to slice through the animal's woolly coat.

Were there other woolly animals?

Yes, plenty. These included a kind of woolly rhinoceros.

This is a woolly rhinoceros. You can tell it is because it looks just like a rhinoceros but has hair.

This mammoth has just heard the hunters coming and is about to make his getaway.

Tusk

What did mammoths taste like?

Mammoth, of course! This probably tasted rather like an elephant (whatever that's like). Our ancestors would have cooked it and not eaten it raw.

Ice Age ice and snow

Were mammoths only hunted for food?

No. Different parts of a mammoth were used for an amazing number of different things. In fact, some of our ancestors actually lived in houses built out of mammoths!

This scene shows a house made from mammoth tusks and bones.

A row of mammoth skulls.

These tusks make a good archway.

Happy hunters

Firewood is very important in such a cold climate.

Animal skin walls

Did you know?

The last mammoths died over 10,000 years ago. But some mammoths' bodies have been found frozen in huge blocks of ice in a very cold place called Siberia.

They were so cold that they didn't rot away.

This picture shows two Russians finding a frozen mammoth.

15

What tools did they use?

All sorts. Hunter-gatherers went after the same food as many animals. They needed weapons to help them get to this food first.

The more people learned, the more types of weapons and tools were invented.

What tools did they use to make the very first tools?

Good question! The very, very first "tools" would have been *found* not made. For example, a small rock could be used as a hammer.

For some reason, this man is digging a hole.

These branches will be used to make weapons.

This girl is making holes in the skin to sew through later.

A perforator

Tools are used to scrape these animal skins clean.

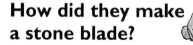
Shaping a piece of stone

How did they make a stone blade?

A type of stone called flint was best for this. It could be chipped into shapes and given a sharp edge.

A piece of flint was given a flat top by hitting it with another stone. This piece is known as the core.

The edge of the core was struck with a bone hammer. This sliced off thin flakes of flint.

These thin flakes were then shaped and sharpened, by carefully chipping the edges with a bone hammer.

16

Did they really carry big wooden clubs?

A large piece of wood might have been useful to use as a club, but our ancestors had far better weapons. They hunted with spears tipped with points of flint, bone, or even just sharpened wood.

This man is making arrows. They are a new idea.

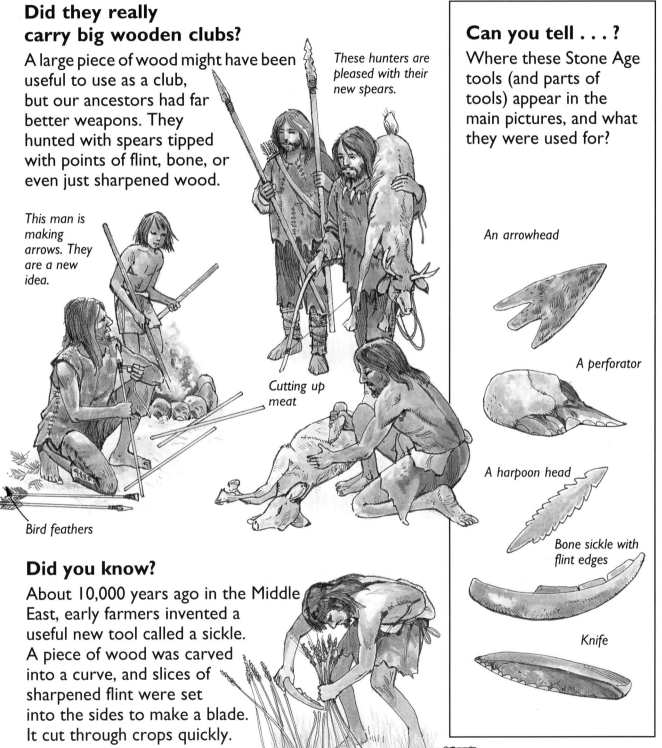

These hunters are pleased with their new spears.

Cutting up meat

Bird feathers

Did you know?

About 10,000 years ago in the Middle East, early farmers invented a useful new tool called a sickle. A piece of wood was carved into a curve, and slices of sharpened flint were set into the sides to make a blade. It cut through crops quickly.

Can you tell . . . ?

Where these Stone Age tools (and parts of tools) appear in the main pictures, and what they were used for?

An arrowhead

A perforator

A harpoon head

Bone sickle with flint edges

Knife

17

There's more on the next page.

Did they only use weapons made of wood and stone?

For a long time, yes. Then, 6,000 years ago, they discovered metals. The first metals used by early people were gold and copper. But they weren't used to make weapons.

These two are blowing on the fire to keep the flames hot. It makes them hot too.

Vessel full of hot melted bronze

Why wasn't gold used for making weapons?

Because a gold arrowhead would have bent! It was too soft, and so was copper. Later, a stronger metal was made from copper and tin. It is called bronze and was turned into everything from swords to pins and knives.

This boy is tying the new bronze spearheads to the shafts. He likes this job.

Part of a cast for making large pins for clothes

Why was bronze a good metal to use?

Because it is very strong but easy to shape. This was done by heating it up until it melted and became a liquid. The liquid was then poured into casts and left to cool into solid shapes.

Pot

Sword

Clothes pins

Head of axe

All of these objects, on the left, are made of bronze. They were made by early farmers, using casts.

Internet link: for a link to a Web site where you can see reconstructions of looms and coiled pots, go to **www.usborne-quicklinks.com**

How did they make most pots?

From clay. The first clay pots were made about 10,000 years ago. They were baked in an open fire to harden them. Later on, special ovens, called kilns, were built to make hotter fires for hardening pots.

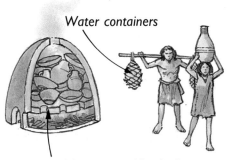

Water containers

Cooking pot

Cook with backache

This is a kiln, a special kind of oven for hardening clay pots.

Frightened mouse

These prehistoric pots have been decorated in very different ways.

Can pots tell us about ancient people?

Yes. Where the pots were found, what they look like and what they were used for all help to build up a picture of everyday life of the time.

Did they have any machines?

A very simple machine, called a loom, was invented about 11,000 years ago. It was used to weave sheep's and goat's wool into cloth.
   Hunter-gatherers didn't have machines.

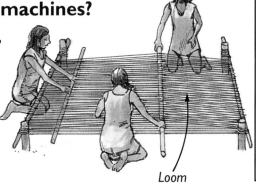

Loom

How can I make a prehistoric pot?

You can't, without going back in time. But you could try making a pot in the same sort of way our ancestors did.

Roll some clay into a ball. Press both thumbs into the middle. Then use your fingers to pull up the sides, as shown below.

Another prehistoric pot was the coil pot. You can make a copy of this type by rolling out long thin "snakes" of clay. Then coil each one into a ring, one on top of the other.

Once you have done that, use your fingers to smooth down the sides and make a pattern.

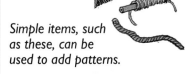

Simple items, such as these, can be used to add patterns.

19

Why was fire so important?

Because it has so many uses. Our earliest ancestors were probably frightened of fire. But, about 500,000 years ago, they realized that fire could be used for heat, light, cooking and protection.

How did they make fire?

Probably by the simplest method there is: banging two stones together to make a spark. A little later, they probably started rubbing pieces of wood to create a flame.

Drill stick

Hearth stick

The tip of this drill stick is rubbed against the hearth stick to make a flame.

Hunters with flaming torches are forcing frightened elephants to run into marshy ground.

How did they know there was fire before they knew how to make it?

Good question! The answer is that fire occurs naturally, and our ancestors would have seen it. For example, lightning hitting a tree or dry grass can cause a fire.

Hundreds of thousands of years ago, hunters like these may have used flaming torches to set fire to grassland to force frightened animals to run into marshy ground.

These hunter-gatherers are certainly hunting and not gathering today.

The seeds from these grasses can also be eaten.

The tusks will be turned into tools.

The skin will be used to make clothing.

The meat will be eaten.

Marshland

This girl would rather be having elephant meat for supper.

Did you know?

In China, there is a cave full of huge piles of 460,000 year-old ash.

Archaeologists believe that the fires in the cave were never put out. These early people probably didn't know how to make their own flame.

How was fire so useful?

Its warmth meant people could move to colder areas. Its light meant that people could stay outside later or go farther into darkened caves. Fire also frightened away dangerous animals. Later, it was used to cook food.

These children are cooking. Cooking is one of the things that makes people different from other animals.

21

How did they understand each other?

In many different ways. The words we speak, read and write have taken thousands of years to turn into what they are today. Our earliest ancestors had to make up everything from nothing.

This handprint was found by a painting on a cave wall. It was probably what the prehistoric artist used as a signature.

The story this man is telling is full of useful hunting hints.

As the number of words grew, people probably gathered in groups, like this one, to tell stories.

Nice and warm near the fire

How did people first talk to each other?

Nobody knows exactly. They probably used a lot of grunts and expressions with their faces. Hand signals would also have been very useful.

Bat-eared fox   Tortoise   Hare   Ostrich

These are some of the hand signals still used by an African tribe to mean certain animals.

Later, *Homo sapiens* would have developed a proper spoken language. We don't know what it was like, because it was never written down. Writing was only invented about 5,500 years ago.

An early example of keeping a record of something.

Many people in this scene are writing things down. See if you can guess what they are recording.

Cutting nicks into a bone

A nosey goat

Why did people need writing?

Writing was only invented once people had settled down to farm. The more people there were in one place, the harder it was to remember who owned what.

Who invented writing?

No single person or single group of people sat down and said: "Hey, let's invent a written language". Writing first developed in Sumer (now part of Iraq) and then, soon after that, in Egypt.

These clay tablets are covered in a very old kind of writing called cuneiform. They are from Sumer, and are about 5,000 years old.

	Pictographic writing	An in-between stage	Cuneiform writing
Bird			
Sun			
Grain			
Ox			
Fish			

The first writing is known as pictographic writing. It used pictures as words. In Sumer, the pictures slowly changed into symbols. Their writing is called cuneiform. "Cuneiform" means wedge-shaped. It was written by pressing a wedge-shaped tip onto clay.

Did they have books?

No. They didn't even have paper to write on. But the remains of an archive built by early farmers was found in a place called Ebla, in what is now Syria.

Over 1,900 clay tablets such as these were found.

Part of Ebla archive might have looked like this.

A chunky librarian hard at work

Clay tablet "books"

Are picture symbols still used today?

Yes. This symbol is used all over the world. Do you recognise it?

If not, find out on page 32.

23

How did they get around?

Most of the time, they walked. Hunter-gatherers needed to get around to find food and shelter. They followed animals when hunting, and moved to different places in different seasons.

Did they have roads?

No, but tracks might have been worn into the ground by people tramping along the same routes. By 10,000 years ago, wooden trackways were sometimes built across marshy ground.

This group has been on the move for days. They are carrying everything they own.

A quick bite to eat

This girl is annoying her mother.

Meat for the next week

These children are playing at hunting.

What if it snowed?

They'd stay at home if they could. It would have been too cold, too difficult and too tiring for weaker members of the family to go far in such bad weather.

Some people probably *had* to go out to find food.

An early skier dressed for action

Did they ride horses?

Not hunter-gatherers. Horses probably weren't tamed until at least 6,000 years ago. Even then, people were more likely to eat them, or use them to pull loads, rather than ride them.

Experts are still puzzling over this horse's head carving. It was carved by hunter-gatherers, but it looks as though it is wearing a harness to be ridden.

Did they use boats?

Yes, from about 55,000 years ago. At first boats were probably just tree trunks. By about 6,000 years ago, there were some proper sailing ships.

This boat is made from half a log, with the wood hollowed out of the middle.

This picture on this pot is of an early ship. The pot is almost 6,000 years old and was made in Egypt.

Cabins

Oars

Paddle

Fishing spear

An unfortunate fish

How did they move heavy things without trucks?

With difficulty! When they wanted to shift things, such as a rock, they made rollers out of tree trunks.

Once the rock had rolled off a roller, the roller could then be put in front of it and used again.

This is certainly a heavy thing! It's a stone for a temple.

These people have turned around to heave this stone uphill.

Didn't they have carts?

Not for a long time. And for a very good reason. No one had invented the wheel until almost 5,500 years ago.

The first carts had solid wheels made from circles of wood cut from tree trunks. Later, metal rims were added to them to make them stronger.

Wooden rollers

Why was the wheel important?

Because people could move faster, and take more with them. For example, a donkey can carry three times as much in a cart as it can on its back.

This clay model of an Indian cart was made about 5,500 years ago.

25

How did farming change their lives?

Completely and utterly. When farming started about 11,000 years ago, people began to settle down. Unlike hunter-gatherers, early farmers could stay in one place. In time, real villages began to grow up.

Did they milk cows?

Not to begin with. Cows were just used for meat. Goats' milk was drunk long before cows' milk. After about 1,000 years (that's about 10,000 years ago), early farmers began to milk cows.

What animals did they keep?

Sheep and goats, to begin with. These were originally hunted by people of the Middle East, who later became the first farmers. From about 10,000 years ago, pigs and cows were kept too.

Earth for building a new house

Builders busy building

—This cow is quite happy staying where it is.

This dog is pleased to see its master.

This picture shows what an early Middle Eastern farming settlement might have looked like.

An unsafe-looking ladder

These people are drying fruit.

The laziest person on the farm

Which crops did they grow?

Wheat and barley, at first. These were once wild grasses. Farmers would have collected the seeds and planted them. They soon discovered which plants made the best grain.

This person is milking a goat.

These people are making pots.

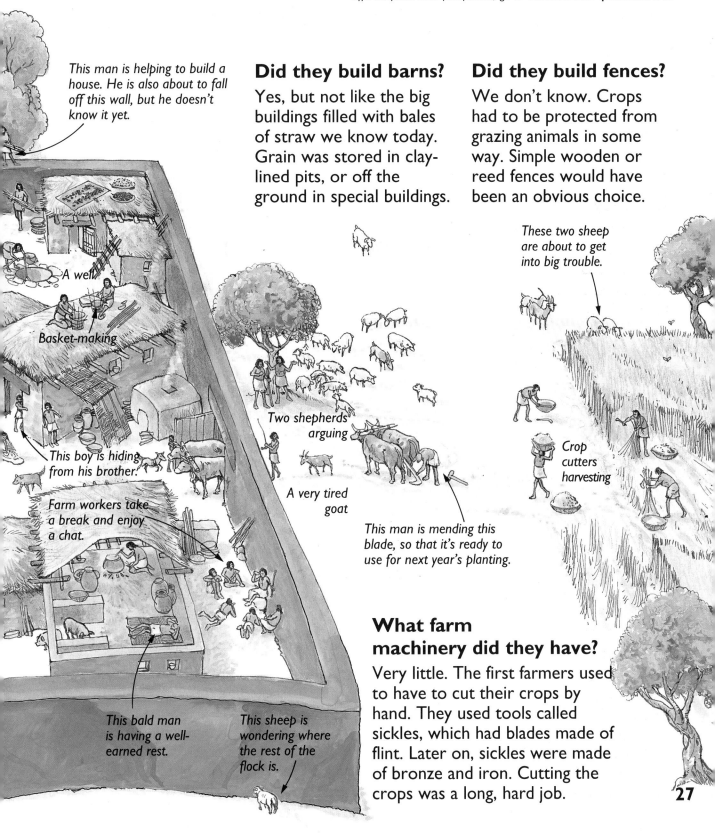

*Internet link: for a link to a Web site where you can click on a map to find out where different foods were first farmed, go to **www.usborne-quicklinks.com***

This man is helping to build a house. He is also about to fall off this wall, but he doesn't know it yet.

Did they build barns?

Yes, but not like the big buildings filled with bales of straw we know today. Grain was stored in clay-lined pits, or off the ground in special buildings.

Did they build fences?

We don't know. Crops had to be protected from grazing animals in some way. Simple wooden or reed fences would have been an obvious choice.

These two sheep are about to get into big trouble.

A well

Basket-making

This boy is hiding from his brother.

Farm workers take a break and enjoy a chat.

Two shepherds arguing

A very tired goat

This man is mending this blade, so that it's ready to use for next year's planting.

Crop cutters harvesting

This bald man is having a well-earned rest.

This sheep is wondering where the rest of the flock is.

What farm machinery did they have?

Very little. The first farmers used to have to cut their crops by hand. They used tools called sickles, which had blades made of flint. Later on, sickles were made of bronze and iron. Cutting the crops was a long, hard job.

27

Did they believe in God?

Our ancestors probably believed in many different gods and goddesses. Anything which seemed magic would have been seen as a god - from the Sun and Moon to fire, wind and water.

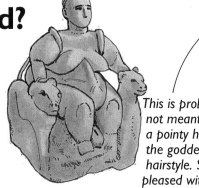

This is probably not meant to be a pointy hat, but the goddess's hairstyle. She looks pleased with it.

How do we know about their gods?

From the clues archaeologists have found. In the Middle East, a number of small stone and clay figures have been discovered with huge staring eyes. Archaeologists believe that these are models of some of their early gods.

A pretty frightening model of a staring god, found in Yugoslavia.

Many ancient carvings are figures of very large females, such as these. Some experts think that these are models of a great Mother Goddess.

A burial is taking place. There is music and dancing from the dead people's friends.

This man is in charge.

Friends bring presents.

Food, tools, and weapons for their journey to the next life

This man is making plenty of noise with his mammoth's skull drum. He goes to all the funerals.

Did our ancestors bury their dead?

Sometimes, but people were also cremated or left in rivers. Early farmers sometimes put piles of earth over the top of the grave, to mark the spot.

Simple hollow wooden pipe

Did they believe in heaven?

It seems so. People were often buried with the tools and weapons they were thought to need on the journey to a new life. Some bodies were also buried with food.

*Internet link: for a Web site where you can find out more about excavations and discoveries at Çatal Hüyük, go to **www.usborne-quicklinks.com***

Did they have ceremonies?

Yes. There is plenty of evidence of religious ceremonies from the time of the early farmers about 10,000 years ago. Archaeologists have even found clues to suggest that hunter-gatherers had ceremonies too.

Where did they pray?

At first, deep inside caves and, later, in clearings in woods and forests.

When people began to settle down, the first shrines and temples were built.

A painted statue of a goddess

This is a priest. He is wearing a leopard skin.

The poor leopard's paw

Three priestesses of different ages

Oldest   Youngest

Offerings of food and drink for their goddess

This is what a shrine might have looked like in a place called Çatal Hüyük, now in Turkey, 8,000 years ago.

What were the first temples like?

Very different from each other - from temple pyramids in what is now Peru, to underground rooms in Malta.

This is what the temples of Tarxien in Malta might have looked like 5,000 years ago.

Most important temple

Thatched roofs

Stone walls

29

What goes on at an archaeological dig?

The word "archaeology" means "the study of everything ancient". On a dig, archaeologists try to build up an idea of how people lived in the past. They do this from the clues our ancestors left behind.

Archaeologists work like detectives, gathering evidence from the remains of pottery, bones, pollen, insects, buildings and whatever else they find.

A small archaeological dig. Here archaeologists, students and volunteers work together.

This man isn't looking where he's going.

Pickaxes and wheelbarrows are used for shifting soil.

This student has poured rubble on her foot.

This archaeologist is very carefully scraping away the soil with a tiny tool.

These human skulls are an exciting find.

Our ancestors didn't live underground, so why do we have to dig to find their homes?

Because soil is made up of the trees and plants which have died and rotted over millions of years. This means that ground level is much higher today.

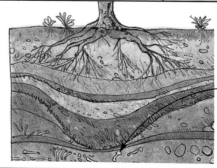

These bones have been covered by rotting plants turned to soil.

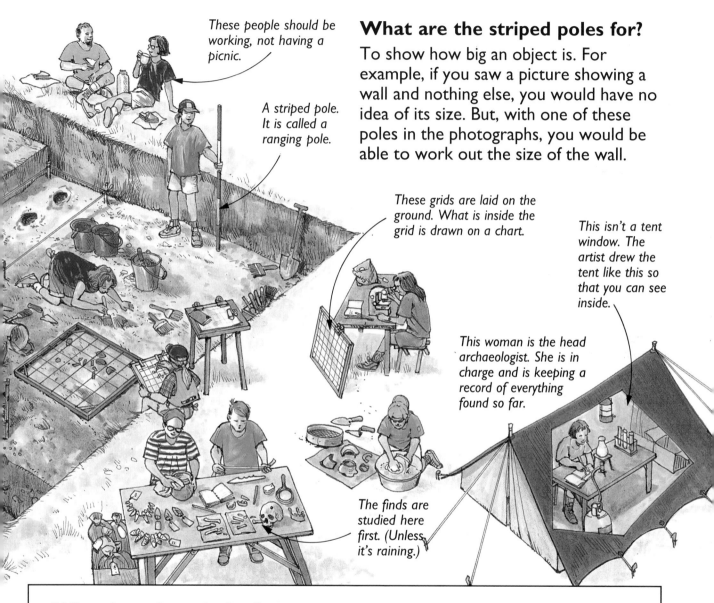

These people should be working, not having a picnic.

A striped pole. It is called a ranging pole.

These grids are laid on the ground. What is inside the grid is drawn on a chart.

This isn't a tent window. The artist drew the tent like this so that you can see inside.

This woman is the head archaeologist. She is in charge and is keeping a record of everything found so far.

The finds are studied here first. (Unless it's raining.)

What are the striped poles for?

To show how big an object is. For example, if you saw a picture showing a wall and nothing else, you would have no idea of its size. But, with one of these poles in the photographs, you would be able to work out the size of the wall.

What is carbon dating?

A way of telling the age of certain remains. Living things, such as plants, animals and people, contain something called carbon 14. When they die, the amount of carbon 14 in them gets less. Experts can measure the amount of it in what they're studying. They can then tell its age.

According to carbon dating, this piece of an ancient carving is thought to be 20,000 years old.

31

Index

32

Answers

Page 9.
The animals in the cave painting are supposed to be a horse and a cow.
Page 17.
All the answers are in the pictures and labels. Look carefully!
Page 23.
The symbol is a warning that something is radioactive.

First published in 1994 by Usborne Publishing Ltd, 83-85 Saffron Hill, London ECIN 8RT, England. www.usborne.com Copyright © 2002, 1994 Usborne Publishing Ltd. The name Usborne and the devices 🔱 🎈 are Trade Marks of Usborne Publishing Ltd. All rights reserved. No part of this publication may be reproduced, stored in a retrieval system, or transmitted in any form or by any means, electronic, mechanical, photocopying, recording or otherwise, without the prior permission of the publisher. Printed in Belgium.

Usborne Publishing is not responsible, and does not accept liability for the availability or content of any Web site other than its own, or for any exposure to harmful, offensive, or inaccurate material which may appear on the Web. Usborne Publishing will have no liability for any damage or loss caused by viruses that may be downloaded as a result of browsing the sites it recommends.